The

Of Prophecy

by

Norvel Hayes

(Volume number seven of a nine part series on The Gifts Of The Spirit.)

HARRISON HOUSE
P.O. Box 35035
Tulsa, Okla. 74135

(All Scripture quotations in this volume are from *The King James Version* of the Bible, unless otherwise stated.)

". . . to another prophecy. . ."
(I Corinthians 12:10).

ISBN 0-89274-145-7
Copyright © 1980 by Norvel Hayes
Printed in the United States of America
All Rights Reserved

Table of Contents

4

1

God Would Not Have You Ignorant

The nine *gifts of the Spirit* are recorded in the Bible, by Paul, through the inspiration of the Holy Ghost. God gives these gifts to the *Body of Christ*, and to individuals through the Holy Ghost that lives within them. And God does not want you to be ignorant of those gifts. We read in First Corinthians 12:1-12; "Now concerning spiritual gifts, brethren, *I would not have you ignorant*. Ye know that ye were Gentiles, carried away unto these dumb idols, even as ye were led. Wherefore I give you to understand, that no man speaking by the Spirit of God calleth Jesus accursed: and that no man can say that Jesus is the Lord, but by the Holy Ghost. Now there are diversities of gifts, but the same Spirit. And there are differences of administrations, but the same Lord. And there are diversities of operations, but it is the same God which worketh all in all. But the manifestation of the Spirit is given to every man to profit withal. For to one is given by the Spirit *the word of wisdom;* to another *the word of knowledge* by the same Spirit; To another *faith* by the same Spirit; to another *the gifts of healing* by the same Spirit; To another *the working of miracles;* to another *prophecy;* to another *discerning of spirits;* to another *divers kinds of tongues;* to another the *interpretation of tongues:* But all these worketh that one and the selfsame Spirit, dividing to every man severally as he will. For as the body is one, and hath many members, and all the members of that one body, being many, are one body: so also is Christ."

We are going to take a closer look at *the gift of prophecy* in this volume. You may say, "Well, I don't necessarily need prophecy."

Yes you do. *The gift of prophecy* will change your whole life. *The gift of prophecy* is just like the rest of the spiritual gifts. It is a single gift. It sits there by itself. But it is a gift that works hand in hand, sometimes, with the gifts of tongues, and interpretation. Like the gift of faith, and the gift of discerning of spirits, and the others; one manifestation from the Holy Ghost of any of these gifts can change the course of your entire life. It is so important that you know this that God had it recorded in the Bible.

THE GIFT OF PROPHECY IS GIVEN BY THE HOLY GHOST . . .

You cannot prophesy just because you wish to. Perhaps you have been to a lot of those little meetings—home prayer meetings, where everybody in the house prophesied. One will say something, and another person will say something, etc. That is not the *gift of prophecy*. I am not saying that the words that are said, and you hear them, are not from God. They may come from God. But *the gift of prophecy* is when words of English are given to an individual's spirit, by the Holy Spirit—as the Spirit wills. And words of English in a known language begin to boil up out of your spirit, supernaturally. That is when *the gift of prophecy* comes into operation.

I am not saying that you are not supposed to speak out the words that God gives you: giving out words of exhortation and words to build people up are all right. But, if you are just standing there praising the Lord, and you just have some good thoughts—things that you know, and believe that God would have you speak out, that is all right. Those are words of exhortation, and

6

very close to it, but it is not really the spiritual *gift of prophecy*.

The spiritual *gift of prophecy* comes boiling out of an individual, and sometimes, it will nearly lift you out of your seat. It builds up, and it comes to you supernaturally. Words of exhortation, or speaking out words are good, and they are from the Lord. But always remember, every one of the *gifts of the Spirit*, are manifested supernaturally. The *gift of prophecy* boils up out of you, supernaturally, and when you speak it out the people know that it is supernatural. *The gift of prophecy* edifies or builds you up in God. It builds up the Church—in God. So do not be ignorant of *the gift of prophecy*.

The *gift of prophecy* comes as the Spirit wills, and if it boils up out of you, and you refuse to give it out, that grieves the Lord. I have had God angry with me when I didn't want to prophesy. I have, sometimes, begged Him, "Please God; have mercy on me, Jesus." I have thought that I was going to die. When God gives you something to prophesy, He gives it to you supernaturally, and He wants His Word spoken out. I believe that that is the way that the Bible was written. I imagine that God's Word boiled up in Paul when He gave Paul three-fourths of the New Testament. When you read the Bible, you know that it is impossible for just a human being to write its contents. There never has been a human that smart.

Just think about the *Psalms*, and all of the *New Testament*.

The Bible makes Shakespeare look like an amateur. And William Shakespeare probably has received more respect than any other writer in the world, as far as a natural writer is concerned. When the Holy Ghost begins to give out words, and to write words, Shakespeare cannot compare with Him. You can read some of the

Psalms and just get lost in another world. Sometimes I read the letters that Paul wrote to the church, and God comes in my room so strong that I just lie there and weep and cry, and get blessed and shout, and rejoice. I get so far out in God that I have to turn everything off and get back in the natural, so I won't go to heaven. God has come to me when I was in bed, and He has just shaken me and blessed me for three or four hours. He did this to me once, for about two days. And I said, "Lord, I hate to ask You, but if You don't stop blessing me, I am not going to be able to get my work done."

The gift of prophecy brings great blessings to the whole Body of Christ.

Sometimes, the Holy Ghost will bring blessings to an entire congregation at one time. The beautiful part about the *gift of prophecy* is it has its own unique way of working and bringing blessings from heaven to the people. It can bring blessings to any number of people at one time. Once I was at a convention for the *Full Gospel Businessmen's Fellowship International*, in Denver, Colorado. I was just sitting there, and somebody was speaking. Suddenly *the gift of prophecy* began to boil up out of me. This happened when 5,000 people were sitting there. It was so strong that I didn't even have to go to the microphone. When the man stopped speaking I stood up and gave out the prophecy. I couldn't believe that it was me.

Brother Kenneth E. Hagin was sitting in the congregation, and he said, "Boy! Norvel, I tell you, that blasted against the wall."

I said, "I know it, Brother. It didn't even sound like me." I could not believe that it was coming out of me.

8

God will give you a loud voice when there are 5,000 people that He wants to prophesy to.

The manifestation of the *gift of prophecy* is given to the *Body of Christ* in order that it can receive blessings from heaven: so that you can receive profits. We read verse seven again: "But the manifestation of the Spirit is given to every man to profit withal." You will receive profit from the manifestation of the *gift of prophecy*.

If the *gift of prophecy* starts boiling up inside you in public assembly, it is necessary that you speak it out. But God may never call you to prophesy in public. It can just boil up in your own private prayer life. You can be riding down the road in your car, and prophecy can come out of you. Prophecy can be used in you own family. But if *the gift of prophecy* operates in you, it is by the Holy Ghost who lives within you.

The Lord once told me, not to prophesy in churches unless I receive the pastor's permission. I am only telling you what He told me. But—if you know that it is all right for you to prophesy then go ahead. You do not have to worry about anything when it is of God. It will work out right. The peace of God will be there, and everybody will be built up.

BE SURE IT IS OF GOD

You should always be certain that the prophecy is of God. Don't ever worry about putting the things of God to a test. Because you need to be aware that there are familiar spirits that may want you to prophesy. I am sure that you have heard familiar spirits many times, and you could have thought that it was of God. Familiar spirits will come and imitate prophecy, and you have to watch that. If you are just thinking something in your head, do not speak it out. If it is of God, just allow it to boil up out of you. It is then that it builds up the congregation, and it builds you up.

Let's look at the listing of the spiritual gifts again: "For to one is given by the Spirit *the word of wisdom;* to another *the word of knowledge* by the same Spirit; To another *faith* by the same Spirit; to another *the gifts of healing* by the same Spirit; to another *the working of miracles;* to another *prophecy;* to another *discerning of spirits;* to another *divers kinds of tongues;* to another *the interpretation of tongues:* But all these worketh that one and the selfsame Spirit, dividing to every man severally as he will. For as the body is one, and hath many members, and all the members of that one body, being many, are one body: so also is Christ" (vv. 8-12). Going down to verse 18: "But now hath God set the members every one of them in the body, as it hath pleased him. And if they were all one member, where were the body? But now are they many members, yet but one body. And the eye cannot say unto the hand, I have no need of thee: nor again the head to the feet, I have no need of you" (vv. 18-21).

God wants the *Body of Christ* not to be ignorant of the spiritual gifts. Read 1 Corinthians 12:1 again. "Now concerning spiritual gifts, brethren, I would not have you ignorant." If God uses you in the manifestation of the gift of healing, or the gift of faith, or some of the power gifts, you will have a good walk with God. You will become a dedicated Christian. But you will never get to the point where you do not need *the gift of prophecy* in your life. You must never get to the point that you do not hunger after *the gift of prophecy.* You should never get to the point that you do not want somebody who is of God to prophesy to you. God would not have you ignorant . . . .

2

What is Prophecy?

Prophecy is when God manifests himself supernaturally to the spirit of man. He puts words into man's spirit, in a known language. Prophecy is used by God to bring a great message.

Prophecy is not manifested in the same way as *the gift of tongues*, and *interpretation*. If you are to prophesy, God gives words to you in a known language. It boils up supernaturally inside to one who is to give the prophecy. In other words, prophecy comes out of your spirit supernaturally, as it is given to you by the Spirit of God. When God chooses to use an individual, He releases His power into the person's spirit, and He creates words in a known language.

There is the office of a prophet, and there are those whom God chooses to prophesy at times.

Brother Kenneth E. Hagin is a true prophet of God. In other words, he is divinely called of God to prophesy to *the Body of Christ*. If he doesn't do that he is in trouble with God. He got into trouble with God once, because he refused to prophesy so much. Sometimes, God will put several words in Brother Hagin's spirit. And at other times He will only give him two or three words, and he has to step out on faith to receive the rest of the prophecy.

I am not called to prophesy like Brother Hagin. I am called to be a Bible teacher. And even though *the gift of*

11

prophecy operates through me, as a teacher, I may go for a month and never prophesy. At other times, *the gift of prophecy* will come upon me and I will prophesy from three to five times in one week. *The gift of prophecy comes to me in three ways.*

Number one — God himself will boil words up out of my spirit supernaturally, and it will come piling out of my spirit like an explosion; full of power.

Number two — Like it sometimes happens to Brother Hagin, I will only receive two, or three words, and I have to step out on faith. I don't really like to get it that way, but if that is the way that God chooses to use me, that is fine. I really prefer for *the gift of tongues* to operate through me, and then somebody else can give *the interpretation.*

It is not bad when I have to step out on faith in a home prayer meeting. But when I was sitting in that convention with 5,000 people, including four or five hundred ministers sitting out there—all filled with the Holy Ghost, I had better have received it from God. Because if I had missed it I would have been called on the carpet.

Number three — Sometimes I will be sitting in a place, and somebody will be singing. The Holy Ghost will use anointed songs. Or somebody will be preaching the gospel, and I will just be sitting there listening, and all of a sudden God will give me the whole prophecy, from the beginning to the end. It will be something that I have never known or heard before. But I will know it from the beginning to the end. It is like I know the story of *Goldilocks and the Three Bears* . . . . That story has been in my spirit since I was a small child: I know that story. All of a sudden, "Sw-o-o-o-sh!" God has put that

12

entire prophecy down in my spirit. I know it from beginning to the end, supernaturally.

I have learned that when God does that it is always to build up the congregation. It is always given to complement the message. Usually the prophecy will contain the Scriptures that the person is speaking on, or to complement them.

Sometimes I will just be sitting there, and I begin to see a picture—like a mini-vision. The prophecy will begin to boil up out of my spirit, and I will speak out what I see in the picture. Nobody knows that I have seen anything except myself.

VISIONS ARE SCRIPTURAL

A vision is a scene or picture that God shows an individual by His Spirit, that the individual has never seen before. In other words the scenes are given to him (or her) supernaturally, by the Spirit of God.

When this happens to me *a word of knowledge*, and prophecy will begin to boil up inside my spirit, and I will prophesy out what I see. I have never seen it before. Here—two gifts of the Spirit are involved—*the word of knowledge*, and *the gift of prophecy* through the vision.

You may say, "Brother Norvel, is all this stuff real? Do you really get prophecy three different ways?"

Yes. It is real. Brother Kenneth E. Hagin says that he gets most of the prophecy about two or three words at a time. I thank God that He gave that to Brother Hagin. He said that he had to go through several battles with God to get bold enough to get up and speak it out like that.

13

Prophecy is important. Prophecy is used by God to bring a great message. God puts words into man's spirit, in a known language, for the building up and edifying of a person or an entire congregation.

3

The Gift of Prophecy in Operation

Several years ago I was sitting on the platform in an *Assembly of God Church,* in Brownsburg, Indiana. I was getting ready to teach the Bible when I looked up and saw Brother Hagin and his wife walking in. The pastor came over to me and said, "Did I see Kenneth Hagin come in here and sit down?"

I said, "Yeah, that's right. Brother Hagin and his wife have been in town, on a radio rally. They have the night off, and they have come out to hear me speak."

He said, "Can you believe that Kenneth Hagin has come to my church?"

I said, "Yeah, I believe it. He is sitting right there."

The pastor said, "I know, Brother Norvel, you know him real well. And you know that we have lots of food fixed for you, over at the parsonage tonight, after the service. How about you inviting him and his wife to come over to the parsonage after service, and enjoy fellowship? I have been wanting to get some of his material for my Sunday School department. And I want to talk to him about what would be the best."

I said, "Okay. I will ask him when the service is over . . . ."

We went to the parsonage after the service, and Brother Hagin was sitting there talking to the pastor. I was sitting there talking to Oretha, and I had no idea that anything was going to happen. We were just sitting and talking about the good things of the Lord, and how the Lord was leading them. Mrs. Hagin said, "You know, the Lord wants to use us, Brother Norvel, to bless a few young fellows and young women who have been called into the ministry. We feel like the Lord is going to give us a room that will hold twenty or thirty students. Never more than forty or fifty chosen vessels, that God has anointed to preach the gospel. God wants to share our knowledge of Him, and what we have learned over the years . . . ."

Suddenly, as Oretha Hagin was talking to me, I began to see a campus (on the inside of me). I just began to see it in my spirit. It was not just two or three buildings, but many buildings, on acres and acres of ground. The vision of that campus started boiling up out of me so strong, and the words started boiling up out of me. And I just spoke it out right there in the living room of that *Assembly of God parsonage.*

That got Brother Hagin's attention! And it so blasted her, that when I finished she shook her head. She believed it, but she started to rebel against it. She said, "Oh no! oh no! No, Norvel. We don't want anything like that. We just want one little room somewhere that will hold twenty or thirty students—not over forty or fifty, that the Lord wants us to help and bless. The Lord wants us to bless them, Brother Norvel. We don't want anything like that."

I said, "Of course I know what I know by the Holy Ghost that is within me. I know what I saw. And I know, that I know, that I know. He gave it to me." I knew how it was boiling up out of me supernaturally—in my spirit. And I knew that it was *the gift of prophecy.* I saw it, and I said, "Oretha, it doesn't make any difference what you want. That is what you are going to get, anyway."

16

She said, "Oh no, oh no, oh no!"

I said, "Look for a campus. It is coming."

Of course, Brother Hagin had not even dreamed about *Rhema Bible Training Center*, much less believed that he would be in charge of a campus. He thought that he was going to get one little room, and train a few people who were anointed of God. But I saw *Rhema Bible Training Center*, on the inside of me.

A few years later I was walking across the campus with Brother Hagin, and he said, "Well, Brother Norvel, see all this stuff going up here. This is what you saw."

I said, "Not all of it! Brother Hagin, you are just getting started good. Understand that! You are just getting started good." As he watches *R.B.T.C.* grow by the year it shocks him. I don't believe that he has received the full picture of it.

I believe that I am the only one who has the full picture. You know, we have board meetings, and camp meetings, and talk about how we are going to have to build another building, and that it will cost a million dollars to build it. And I just sit there, and on the inside of me I go, "Ha-ha-ha-ha! Oh yes, Brother Hagin, just brave on! Is that right? Oh, you have to raise some money to build a building? Well, Brother Hagin, you have lots of buildings coming yet. And you may as well get ready."

You may say, "Well, why doesn't God just show it to Brother Hagin?"

Well, God loves Brother Hagin. And one or two buildings at a time is about all one man can stand. God doesn't want to drive him nuts. If he had shown him that campus, and said, "Look at this. You are going to be in charge of *Rhema Bible Training Center*. And I am holding you responsible to build all of it;" what do you think would have happened?

He would have gone, "Ugh-h-h-h!" because he does not think businesswise. That is the reason that God sent Reverend Doyle (Buddy) Harrison, and others to him. He needs some helpers who know something about business.

Understand this. God will get *Rhema Bible Training Center* built. You can mark that down in your book.

I was talking about this, and the following poetic prophecy came from God, through Buddy Harrison, concerning *R.B.T.C.*

"For many things be hard to the flesh for in that you
find no rest.
As so there is a withdrawing of the natural man.
But the spiritual man will always be able to stand.
And you will arise upon that occasion,
And say, 'Yes, the Lord did give me this visitation.
And yes, it will be a solid place.
Oh, it will be built by God's glorious grace!'
And it will be fulfilling unto the Lord.
And that way, to man, it will not be hard.
For he must walk one step at a time;
For in that he will find God's plan divine.
And oh, there will always be glorious light;
And then it will be pleasing in men's sight.
And so, there will be rest and refreshing that surely
come to pass,
Because the glory of God, and the Spirit of God shall
cause the school to prosper, and to last."

The above is the gift of prophecy that was given to Reverend Harrison, as I stood in the pulpit. The Spirit of God flowed from Buddy to me. That day the people saw *the gift of prophecy* in manifestation as I taught on the subject.

18

4
The Importance of the Gift of Prophecy

In Old Testament times most prophecy was foretelling. But today, God not only uses prophecy to foretell, but to build up the church. *The Body of Christ* longs to hear from God. And *the gift of prophecy* is the number one way that God talks to His Spirit-filled children. *The gift of prophecy* is given to build up *the Body of Christ* in God. It is for the edification of the church. And the New Testament church needs to be built up. That is the reason that you need to go to church every time the doors are open.

You can hear an anointed song, and it will open up your spirit to listen to God's Word. The singing ministry has been deflated for years. And the church has never learned that when the singing ministry comes from God, it is powerful.

It is important that the gifts of the Spirit operate in the church. The Holy Ghost will come in so strong, and give you things. He will heal you, and set you free.

The gift of prophecy is very important in my life.

How does *the gift of prophecy* work, and what is the importance of it? I will give you a personal example. Several years ago I set up a meeting for Brother Kenneth E. Hagin, in Cleveland, Tennessee. At that time I owned six different restaurant businesses. Everything was going fine, and I was having no financial problems.

Brother Hagin was speaking one night, and I was sitting back in the congregation, because I like to be fed when people like Brother Hagin come around. As he was speaking, all of a sudden he stopped teaching, and began to prophesy. I do not remember everything that he said, but the church took it down, and it has come to pass already. Suddenly in the middle of the prophecy, he called my name.

The moment he called my name, the Spirit of God hit me. It was like somebody just knocked me out of the world in which I was living. And I just broke, and began to weep, and weep, and weep.

God said to me, "The enemy is going to attack your finances, and a dark cloud will come upon your finances. But if you will keep working for me, and be faithful, and you will pray, and pray, and pray, and pray, and pray, and pray, you will come out of this attack. I will bring you out of the attack of the enemy, and you will be more financially successful than you have ever been."

I said, "Attack my finances? I don't have any financial problems . . ." I owned (along with the six restaurants) a manufacturing company, and I had my own sales distributing company. I was making from four to six thousand dollars a week, mostly from the distributing part of the business.

About six months went by, and the sky fell on me. You talk about a dark cloud. **It came upon me.** All of a sudden, three of my restaurant managers turned *flakey*. And they weren't making any money at all.

Then, the Holy Ghost told me to go check the books. I took another fellow with me, and I took the keys to the manufacturing company, so my secretary of seventeen years would not know that I was there. I started checking the books at 11:00 p.m., and I discovered that

20

hundreds and hundreds of orders were sitting there. They were supposed to have been shipped out a month before. I looked in the check book, to check on the deposits, and it was then that I learned that my secretary had stolen so many thousands of dollars. I could see that I was going to have to get some money to even get the orders out that were lying there.

The next morning I went to see a lawyer. I said, "Man, you know my secretary has stolen a bunch of money."

He asked, "What do you want me to do about it?" He went on, "You own an Ohio Corporation, and you know that the state of Ohio has state laws concerning corporations." You see, a corporation is not like a business, or a company. You can do what you want to if you own a company. But there are certain laws that govern a corporation. The lawyer said, "Norvel, you can do whatever you want to. She ought to be put in jail. But I am going to tell you right now, if you press charges against her in the state of Ohio, they will put her in the penitentiary."

I said, "Oh, I don't want her to go to the penitentiary. I have known her for years. How long would she get?"

He said, "She will spend at least two years in the state penitentiary if you press charges against her."

I said, "Well, she got married, and it wasn't long before they both started drinking. And she just took the money out . . . ."

I remembered, Brother Hagin has prophesied to me that the devil was going to attack my finances, and a dark cloud was going to come upon me. And that the Lord had said, "If you will pray, and pray, and pray . . . . ,

21

you will come through it. And I will make you more successful than you have ever been."

The lawyer suggested that because of the condition of the thing that I should sell the corporation. So I just sold the manufacturing company, and got another factory in Memphis, Tennessee, to produce all of my business. I still owned my distributing company, and because I produced so much business through that medium, I could not give it up. It is much better now than it was before.

You may say, "Oh, it is a blessing to own a bunch of businesses."

Yes, it is a blessing to own a bunch of businesses the way mine are now. But it was not a blessing then. It is not a blessing if you own five or six businesses with about four of them not making any profit, and you have to get money from somewhere else to even keep them open. That is a curse. And you have never had a financial curse fall on you until you work all month, and then you have to borrow the money to keep the business going. And you are not receiving anything from it . . . .

This went on for about three years. I kept on praying, and praying, and praying. And I kept my faith built up as I kept on praying. Finally, I asked my present secretary, "After you write your check this week, how much money do you have in the main account?" I really was ashamed to ask her.

She said, "Eighty-five dollars."

My main account should carry at least $10,000, for a low figure. And it really should carry from $15,000 to $30,000 all the time. Because when you have a bunch of businesses, a roof on a building, or an air conditioning system could cost from three to five thousand dollars.

22

Eighty-five dollars was not enough to pay her next week's salary. I said, "Mary Lou, I've got news for you!"

"You have?" she said. I suppose she thought that I was going to give her some money.

I walked over and I said, "Do you see that account? Look at that, Mary Lou. What does that say?"

"Eighty-five dollars," she said.

I said, "I see thousands and thousands of dollars in there, do you understand? Not three or four thousand: I see thousands and thousands of dollars in there."

Mary Lou said, "Hunh?"

I walked the floor in the office, and said, "Thank You, Jesus, thank You Lord, for putting thousands, and thousands, and thousands of dollars in my account, to pay all of my bills, and with lots of money left over to spread the gospel, and to buy me what I want. Glory to God! Thank You Jesus. You know you said in that prophecy, through Kenneth Hagin . . . . And I am saying now, devil, I want you to know that I am going to keep on winning souls, and I am going to take sinners to church, and I am going to pass out tracts. I am going to pass out tracts on planes, and I am going to pass out tracts in airport stations, and I am going to pass out tracts wherever I go. Do you understand that, satan? It makes no difference to me, I am going to keep on going on for God. I am going to keep on being faithful in Jesus' name."

I kept on speaking, and giving my testimony. They would introduce me with a fancy introduction: "He owns six businesses . . . ."

I would think, "If you only knew! Big deal! I own six businesses. I wish I was working at Westinghouse." However, I got up and gave my testimony, and I would pray for everything that didn't move. I would just walk around, like I had good sense; worshipping God, and saying, "Thank You, Lord, for sending in thousands of dollars. I speak success over all of my businesses in Jesus' name."

You say, "How long did you have to do that?"

Well, just turn to chapter five and read on.

5

I Did What God Told Me to Do

After I had been confessing *prosperity* for about one year I grew very strong. I said, "Listen, devil. I am going to keep on going on for Jesus. I am going to pass out tracts. I am going to keep on speaking for God. And I am going to keep doing what God wants me to do. Now listen to me, satan, you dumb devil. I will do it the rest of my life if I eat blackeyed peas and corn bread, and that is all I ever get. Satan, you are a thief, and you have had it. If you think that you are going to knock me out of the box with a few thousand dollars, by trying to rob me, I've got news for you. I don't have dollar marks inside of me. I've got a vision of lost souls dying and going to hell. And I am going to rescue every one of them that I can. I will work for God if I have to preach or pass out tracts in the city dump. In fact, it makes no difference whether I speak, or don't speak, satan. I am going to keep on working for God . . . . . ."

You ask, "How did you ever get out of it?"

I was over in San Antonio, Texas three years later. I had been there ten days; speaking in a different church every morning, and one of the two churches that had brought me to San Antonio during the evening services. It was the last service, and the Lord visited us so strong, and sweet, and people were healed. I rode from San Antonio to Houston, Texas with two missionaries. They were going to take me to the airport. I had not been home in some time, and was anxious to go home. As I sat in their room preparing to leave for the airport in

25

fifteen minutes to fly to Chattanooga, Tennessee, the Spirit of God suddenly fell on me. And these words, in a known language began to boil up out of me. It was a prophecy for me. The Lord said, "Son, I want you to call Brother and Sister Goodwin, and call them now."

Brother and Sister Goodwin were pastors of the *First Assembly of God Church*, in Pasadena, Texas; a suburb of Houston. I had not seen them for five years. I said, "Yes, Lord, that is for me," and I picked up the phone and called them.

Brother Goodwin said, "Oh, Brother Norvel, we haven't seen you in so long. Please, don't leave until you come to see us."

As soon as I walked into the Goodwin house, the devil jumped on their maid. She came out of the kitchen, screaming with pain all over her body, I said, "Oh, no you don't. In Jesus' name, come out of her." I cast that thing off of her. The maid started rejoicing, and she shouted all over the house. The Holy Ghost was working: Sister Goodwin spoke in tongues to me, and Brother Goodwin gave me the interpretation. God said, *"If you will go to Tulsa, Oklahoma for Me, I will show you two things after you get there."* At that time I only knew three people in Tulsa: a millionaire (named Ford), Oral Roberts, and Kenneth Hagin.

I said, "Tulsa, Oklahoma? What for?" I knew Brother Hagin better than I knew the other two. I said, "All right, Lord, I will do it."

I PASSED THE TEST, AND GOD KEPT HIS WORD

When God tells you something it comes straight from heaven. It pays to listen to the Spirit of God, and to obey Him. On the way to Tulsa God moved upon me supernaturally, and showed me how to get my daughter saved. *And I would put that in action when I arrived home.*

I arrived in Tulsa, and was sitting in the den of the Hagin's small apartment. The Lord said, "Go over and lay hands on Oretha. I want to bless her." As I reached out and touched her with the end of my fingers (as the Lord told me to do), Oretha fell flat on the floor; crying, and weeping. When Brother Hagin saw that, he dropped to his knees and began to pray in tongues. He did this for about an hour. After some time, the Lord told me that Buddy (Reverend Doyle Buddy Harrison) was there, and that I could go home. I explained this to Brother Hagin, and he agreed to take me to the airport. On the way to the airport, I said, "Brother Hagin, I prayed so hard in tongues for two or three hours . . . ."

Brother Hagin said, "Norvel, the Lord showed me why He sent you to Tulsa. *He sent you here for two reasons. First, to pray for my wife, and bring a blessing to her. And then, He told me to tell you prophecy.*" The same man who had prophesied to me about a dark cloud that would come upon my business, and that I must keep on praying, and praying, and praying, and that I would come through the attack of the devil, and I would be more financially successful than I had ever been, was going to be used of God to prophesy to me again.

God said, *You have passed My test of faith. And because you have, Son, you obeyed me. And because you have obeyed Me My light is going to shine down from heaven. It is going to break through all the dark clouds, and shine upon you. It is going to shine upon your finances. And it shall come, and come, and come, in abundance to you.*"

I had not seen a financial blessing in three long years. But I had kept on walking steadfast; working for God, and praying. Holding my faith up. Going down to

27

my office, and walking back and forth across the floor, saying, "Thank You, Lord. I see thousands of dollars in my bank account. Thank You, Jesus."

I owned a piece of property at that time, that I had bought several years before for the amount of $13,000. About ten days after that trip to the airport, I received a phone call from a man in Florida who wanted to buy it. I agreed to sell the property for the amount of $28,000. Since we had to get together to complete the deal, I explained this to him: "I am going to have to speak in New York. And I am going to speak at a state convention in Jackson, Mississippi. I will fly from New York to Tampa, and you meet me at the Tampa airport. I will get my reservations to leave on the next plane, and I will fly from Tampa to Jackson." The man had the papers and met me at the airport as we agreed. And when I signed those papers I had made $15,000. Remember: I had not even had a $500 blessing in three years. But I refused to waver in the midst of the storm.

All of my family left me, and I sat in my house, alone for three years. But I did not waver . . . . Do not let anybody talk you out of going to church, or getting involved with God, and prophecy, tongues, and interpretation. Don't let them talk you out of casting out devils, passing out tracts, or bringing sinners to church.

If you will make up your mind that you are going to work for God, you will find that He has many ways that He can reach you.

A car dealer friend of mine, and I had bought a piece of property together. We had paid $15,000 for it. We were in Denver, Colorado, at a *Full Gospel Businessmen's International* convention. We decided to have a prayer meeting. This man is one of America's largest car dealers. He owns insurance companies, and he owns a leasing company that probably has six or seven thousand cars leased out. He doesn't know how much money he is worth. But I knew him in the days when he only had a small dealership, and he worked his way up.

Bill and I were on the floor, praying. And Bill got up and came over, and put his arm around me, as he said, "Norvel, the Lord wants me to give you my part of that property that we own together." He said, "Fix up the papers, and I will give it to you. For some reason, God wants me to give it to you."

We had the papers fixed up, and he signed the property over to me. That happened just a few days before Brother Hagin prophesied to me.

I had $7,500 in that property. And I received a call, wanting to know if I would sell the property. He offered me $87,500 for it. I said, "Well, not really, I wanted $100,000 for it."

The man said, "Well, I have $87,500 if you will take it." I thought about that light that was going to shine from heaven. And I said, "Yeah, I believe I will take it."

I said, "Jesus, what am I going to do with all this money?" as I thought, "One day, $85 in my bank account, and now, $100,000 lying there."

The Lord said, "You are going to spend it for me. Or I am going to take it away from you."

I said, "I will, Lord. Just show me."

He said, "I will." He did, and I did! And the blessings began to flow. Let me just pass this on to you. Prophecy, boiling up out of you supernaturally, will tell you where to go, and what to do, when you don't know where to go or what to do.

I did not know that I was supposed to call the Goodwins. How could I have known that? And how was I supposed to know that God wanted me to go to Tulsa, Oklahoma, when I had my mind set on Chattanooga, Tennessee? When prophecy comes to you from God, through somebody that knows God, and you respect them, it can bring great blessings to you. Not only to you, but to many other people. Can you imagine a word from God bringing a spiritual blessing to Sister Hagin? And causing me to cast the devil out of a maid, and set her free?

The gift of prophecy is important. God can give you something straight from heaven, as He did me, concerning my daughter.

My daughter would come home from the *Playmate Club*, at three or four o'clock in the morning: glassy eyed, and on dope. And there I was, a Bible teacher, going around the country. I would say, "Zona, you came in here at three o'clock in the morning. Honey, now you know better than that . . . . I didn't raise you that way, Sweetheart. Don't you understand?"

God heard all that I was saying to her, and He told me that I had not been loving her as I was supposed to love her. He said, "I want you to tell her two things: tell her that you love her, and that I love her. And then I want you to shut up. When your daughter comes in, don't even ask her where she has been. All that does is just hurt the wound that is already there because you cannot help where she has been."

Did you ever think of that? You cannot help where your children have been. Regardless of whether or not they took ten pills, or drank two fifths of whiskey, and did the *funky-chicken* all night. I obeyed God; I did not even ask her where she had been. I just told her that I loved her, and that God loved her.

30

And God sent an angel into her room, and brought her back to Him. I was obeying prophecy, in my daughter's case.

Parents, listen to me. I got this straight from heaven. Regardless of how you love your children, you can get *all screwed up* in the eyes of God; especially if you are a Christian. God showed me why. He said, *"Son, your spiritual pride is hurt. You are ashamed to have a daughter that goes to night clubs and takes dope."* This is where it got me: *He said, "I never turned against you when you were in sin. Why can't you love your own daughter while she is in darkness, the way I loved you, when you were in darkness? All of those sins you committed boiled up into heaven, in front of me. How do you think I felt?"*

I got away from that harsh, fatherly, protective type of love, and went back to the way that Jesus loved me. After I had done that for six months, my daughter said, "Daddy, I am sick and tired of night clubs. You love me so much, Daddy. And I know that God is in this house. I feel protected here: I feel secure here. You didn't raise a stupid child. I know that every friend that I have is a phony. And I am just as phony as they are. But I know God . . . . I mean I have known the Lord . . . ." God kept His Word concerning my daughter. Praise the Lord! Because I did what He told me to do.

31

6
When God Speaks — Listen!

The *Body of Christ*, as a whole, tends to take the gift of prophecy too lightly. I have seen many churches where the people are *Spirit-filled*, and they are supposed to love God, and basically, they do. But the Holy Spirit will be in operation, through *the gift of tongues*, and He will give instructions to the people through *the interpretation of tongues*. There will be something that He will want that particular church to do at that precise moment. For instance: the Lord will say, "If you will praise Me now, certain things will happen." That word came straight from the throne of God. And the people have just sat back down and done nothing.

I just couldn't believe it when I saw it happen. When God speaks to you by His supernatural power; through prophecy, you had better listen to what He is saying to you. Because He means what He says.

Sometimes, when *the gift of prophecy* boils up in you, it can be for your own benefit. As I have pointed out (concerning my daughter) in another chapter, or to another believer. However—nine times out of ten it is to bring a word directly from God for the benefit of the entire church body. He does this to build up the church. God is a Builder-upper. He never drags His children down. That is the reason that He says in His Word, ". . . let the weak say, I am strong" (Joel 3:10).

The fourteenth chapter of First Corinthians explains to the believer what God thinks about *the gift of*

33

prophecy, and what it does for you. We will read verses 1-5: "Follow after charity, and desire spiritual gifts, but rather that ye may prophesy. For he that speaketh in an unknown tongue speaketh not unto men, but unto God: for no man understandeth him; howbeit in the spirit he speaketh mysteries. But he that prophesieth speaketh unto men to edification, and exhortation, and comfort. He that speaketh in an unknown tongue edifieth himself; but he that prophesieth edifieth the church. I would that ye all spake with tongues, but rather that ye prophesied: for greater is he that prophesieth than he that speaketh with tongues, except he interpret, that the church may receive edifying." If you study the above Scripture, you will know that God considers *the gift of prophecy* of utmost importance to His children.

The following is a prophecy that the Lord gave to the people when I was ending my teaching on *the gift of prophecy*. It is a perfect example of how He wants to build up His people.

". . . I will speak to you. I long to have you hear Me; to do just what I say. It will bring you blessings. Blessings that I long for you to have. If only you will hearken unto My Word; every time I speak. I have longed for a church who would listen. I have longed just to speak to you, and have you hear.

"Lift up your hands, and I will enter in; give me all of you. Lift up your hands, and enter in to Me. Lift up your hands, and touch Me. Touch Me; lift up your heart; I'll meet your need. Lift up your hands, lift them up.

"Oh, it is beginning. It is beginning to work. You think that it is over, but it is just beginning. I desire your minds to be transformed on Me. Lift your hands, and you will see. You see My Spirit shall not leave you. See Me in all My glory. You will see how I love you. How I love you! How I love you. I will make you into the one I want you to be, for Me. Take your rest. Take your rest in Me. Let Me do all I want to do. Learn to be just like Me. . .

"Can't you see, it is Me? Don't hold back. All that needs to go. Go to My love, and cling. Go to My love, and cling. How can it be so good? How can it be so good? Doesn't it feel good, to be in My will?"

Books by Norvel Hayes
published by
HARRISON HOUSE

The Number One Way to Fight the Devil — $ .50
Receive That Power — By Faith — $ .50

GIFTS OF THE SPIRIT SERIES
From Heaven Come God's Weapons for the Church
The Gift of the Word of Wisdom
The Gift of the Word of Knowledge
The Gift of Faith
The Gifts of Healing
The Gift of the Working of Miracles
The Gift of Prophecy
The Gift of Discerning of Spirits
The Gift of Tongues & Interpretation of Tongues

Individual books are $1.25 each.
The entire 9 book series for $10.00

ORDER FROM

HARRISON HOUSE
P. O. Box 35035
Tulsa, Okla. 74135

For a complete listing of books and tapes by Norvel
Hayes write:
Campus Challenge
Box 1379
Cleveland, Tenn. 37311